HOPE BEYOND CURE

DAVID McDONALD

Hope Beyond Cure
© Matthias Media 2013

Matthias Media
(St Matthias Press Ltd ACN 067 558 365)
Email: info@matthiasmedia.com.au
Internet: www.matthiasmedia.com.au
Please visit our website for current postal and telephone contact
information.

Matthias Media (USA)
Email: sales@matthiasmedia.com
Internet: www.matthiasmedia.com
Please visit our website for current postal and telephone contact
information.

ISBN 978 1 922206 44 2

Cover design and typesetting by Lankshear Design.

It's been more than ten years since David McDonald became the Brumbies' team chaplain. In my early years as a player I didn't speak to Dave much. Religion wasn't something I needed in order to be a good player. I know now I was very naïve, not necessarily about the religion part but about what Dave actually offered to the team. Since retiring from playing and becoming a coach, I've spoken to Dave more and more often. He sits in the background not as a crazy stalker, but as a passionate supporter. He's a good listener and down to earth. He's not like your typical chaplain—I don't want to offend your typical chaplain, but he's not.

Dave was admitted to hospital in the first week of December 2011, one week after my mum passed away. She had been diagnosed with stage-4 bowel cancer just six weeks earlier, and given no hope of cure. During those six weeks after her diagnosis, I battled a huge amount of anxiety and spent many sleepless nights. When I wasn't at the hospital, I spent all my time trying to find something that would fix Mum.

As I read Dave's book for the first time, I had to compose myself and dry my eyes on many occasions. I had only ever seen cancer from one side, and I realized I wasn't looking for a fix for Mum—I was looking for hope.

I have found this hope in Dave's book, and in Dave himself.

Stephen Larkham
Head Coach, Brumbies Super Rugby Team, Canberra

Because we're all cancer sufferers or potential cancer sufferers, we all need this book for our present or our future. Dave doesn't pull his punches about his illness; yet he does point to hope. Because it's written from personal experience, not an ivory tower, it's always real and never trite. This book will make you smile, might make you cry, and may just change your life. Make sure you read it.

Carl Laferton
Senior Editor, The Good Book Company, London
Author, *Original Jesus*

This book deals with issues close to my heart, since my mother died of cancer earlier this year. My only complaint is that it was not published a year earlier—it would have been the perfect book for her to read. *Hope Beyond Cure* is a moving and deeply encouraging combination of truth, mature reflection and hope, communicated by someone who has known the pit of despair. Read this book and give it away. Its contents should be shared with every person facing death—which, in the end, includes us all.

Constantine R Campbell
Associate Professor of New Testament, Trinity Evangelical Divinity School, Chicago

Although David is a theologian and pastor, he writes as a fellow human hemorrhaging emotional and physical pain. I've seen firsthand how inoperable cancer stole his future and threatened his hope. If you are doing it tough with illness or hardship, or you just have questions and doubts regarding Jesus, this book is for you. It will not give you pithy, cold and callous answers, but an insightful personal reflection toward real hope beyond cure.

Richard Chin
National Director, Australian Fellowship of Evangelical Students, Sydney

No matter what you believe in, when struck down in your prime by a terminal illness, the reality of our human mortality can hit like a tsunami. *Hope Beyond Cure* is a remarkable story of courage, resilience, belief and the power of faith. David McDonald's story will not only inspire you to rise up against your own affliction and never give up, but more importantly it will challenge you to look beyond the here and now for strength, healing and peace.

Rob Clarke
CEO, Rebels Super Rugby Club, Melbourne

I admire the honesty with which David talks about his journey with terminal cancer. We get not only insight into his tears and fears but the reactions of those around him as well. He also talks honestly about how his cancer challenged his faith—with 1500 students praying for you, it can be hard to grasp why you are not immediately cured! Faith in a miracle can lead to irrational avoidance of reality and pain for the family—but David never falls into that trap. This is a warm and honest story of hope, love and faith on a journey filled with uncertainties.

Prof. Bruce Robinson
Professor of Medicine and cancer researcher, Sir Charles Gairdner Hospital, Perth
Western Australian of the Year 2013-14

This story starts with the words *tumour* and *incurable*. David McDonald heard these words when he became a victim of lung cancer. He takes us through the emotional roller-coaster of his diagnosis and treatment, including the challenges to his Christian faith. Eventually Dave transforms those first horrible words into new words: *faith, hope* and *love.*

This is a moving read, raw and open. It shows the real hope Christians have. But this is also a book for those with no faith— who have cancer or who care for someone who does—because it brings intensely practical insights to this modern scourge. I highly recommend reading it at least a couple of times.

Dr David Bell
Medical Oncologist, Royal North Shore Hospital, Sydney

Can anything good come out of cancer?
I have watched David McDonald deal with the most significant and unwanted challenge of his life. In these pages he opens his heart about the journey this has taken him on. It's raw, it's real, and yet Dave manages to bring into light the surprising power of this thing called hope—true hope. I have

seen God at work in his life and I can honestly say my friend is more hope-filled than I can ever remember. His journey shows us why, and his story will speak to all of us.

Marcus Reeves
Senior Pastor, Crossroads Christian Church, Canberra

ABOUT THE AUTHOR

David McDonald had been in Christian ministry for more than two decades—as a pastor of Crossroads Christian Church and a chaplain to the Brumbies Super Rugby Team—until a diagnosis of stage-4 lung cancer shook his world. Dave is an avid sports fan and loves spending time in the outdoors with his family. He blogs at macarisms.com and lives in Canberra with his wife, Fiona, and their younger children.

For Fiona, Marcus, Grace,
Matt, Elizabeth, Luke, Sharon,
and Liam

THANK YOU

I have so much to give thanks for.

I thank God especially for my wonderful wife, Fiona. I'm grateful for her generous love, partnership and support, as well as for her continuous research into my cancer and the possibilities for treatment. And I thank God for my children, Luke and Sharon, Matt and Elizabeth, Grace, and Marcus, and I thank them for their love and generous support and encouragement. While my family's world has been turned inside out and upside down, they have encouraged me as they too have learned to keep their trust in God.

I thank God for my father and mother, Norman and Ruth, who have shared the cancer journey and supported me in prayer and wisdom—often from the other end of the telephone. And I thank God also for the rest of my family and so many friends who have supported me through prayer and practical displays of love and kindness.

I thank God for my home church, Crossroads—for their prayer and practical support and for the opportunity to resume ministry among them. I thank God for good friends all over the world who have prayed, visited, called and written words of love and care, as well as for individuals, churches, and groups who have never met me but have prayed faithfully for me.

I thank God for the medical staff watching over me on this journey—Bill Burke, John Tharion, Desmond Yip, David Bell, Melissa, Maureen, Kate, and so many others.

I thank God for Tara, my editor, who has worked hard to help me communicate this message more clearly.

I thank God that you are reading this book.

Above all, I give thanks to our great God who has shown me such mercy. I thank him for answering the prayers of so many by extending my life and reminding me of the hope of eternity.

David McDonald
October 2013

CONTENTS

INTRODUCTION

"Cancer-free to no hope in less than two weeks."

I found this headline on a cancer forum recently. How, you might ask, could things change so quickly? The truth is, they hadn't. There had been a bad case of miscommunication.

I have cancer, so I browse these forums from time to time. I can't do it every day because I find it too sad, too overwhelming. People are sick, confused, powerless, dying—and, so often, they're completely lacking in hope. Every day there are desperate cries of anguish, pleas for prayer, outpourings of grief. Sometimes there's an explosion of anger at the merciless killer, cancer.

Reading the headline above helped me to clarify exactly what it is that I want this book to achieve. My goal is to shine a light on hope *beyond* a cure.

Don't get me wrong. I'm 100% pro-cure. I long for my cancer to completely disappear. I pray that it will, and I pray the same for others. Medical advances and new discoveries excite me. I love hearing that someone with cancer no longer has any evidence of disease. And I love the possibilities of a new start, with a new outlook, that come with this pronouncement.

Yet when the prognosis is bad, when all attempts at medical intervention have been exhausted, when prayers have not been answered as we might wish—what then? Is there still hope?

Is *cure* the ultimate hope for people with a terminal illness? Is this what seriously ill patients around the world long for above all else? I don't know, really. I haven't asked enough people. My guess is that we have a range of hopes. But this hope founded on cure worries me. If we hang everything on finding a cure and it doesn't happen, what then?

What gives cancer patients the motivation to get out of bed each day, knowing that more pain awaits? And how do those caring for cancer patients—spouses, children, parents, friends—hold on to hope when, despite their best efforts, all they can do is watch helplessly as their loved ones suffer? How does anyone endure when life is painful and difficult and only getting worse? Can we find hope in anything less than a cure? And, more importantly, *is* there hope beyond cure?

Sometimes people are cured from serious illnesses. Some get to celebrate the wonderful news that there is no further evidence of disease. I long for the day when I can say that I've been in remission for a year, or five, or ten, or more. But the reality is that we're all likely to get sick again. It might be the recurrence of cancer or something else altogether. We may recover, and we might keep recovering, but there will come a day when we won't. Death will catch up with each of us eventually.

What, then, of hope? Is it ultimately meaningless? Or is there hope in the face of death? And if there is such a hope, does it change how we live? These are crucial questions, and yet so often people don't ask them. The details of everyday life consume all of us in such a way that we don't pause to consider the bigger picture or the inevitability of our own death. I may not have cancer when I die, but I will still die. Is there hope for me—or for any of us?

I've asked these questions at different points in my life, but since my diagnosis I've asked them with a different urgency and intensity. And I've found that the Bible still answers these questions with a resounding "Yes!" There is hope beyond death, and it's found in Jesus Christ. Since my diagnosis I've journeyed back through the Bible and the foundations of my faith as I've struggled with fear and doubt. This book chronicles some of that journey because—even if you are facing terminal illness—I want you to find encouragement and embrace the real hope that is found only in God. God offers this hope, a hope that stands on the evidence of Jesus' resurrection from the dead, to every one of us—to those who are terminally ill as well as to those who are in full health. If Jesus is alive today, then there is hope beyond death. Death will not have the final say because there is hope beyond cure. I know, because I am living in this hope.

1 HOPELESS

Two devastating words, spoken to me by different people in the same week of December 2011, left me feeling hopeless and lost. *Tumour* and *incurable*. These cruel words took my breath away and ushered in the darkest period of my life. They introduced me to all manner of fears and doubts, shattered my plans and dreams, devastated my family, and challenged my faith in God. These two words changed everything.

I'm fifty years old and enjoying my thirtieth year of marriage to Fiona. We have four children—two boys, followed by a girl, and then another boy. The older boys are married and we are eagerly anticipating the birth of our first grandchild. I live in Canberra, Australia, where I've been working as the pastor of Crossroads Church for nearly two decades. I love my job because it's all about helping people to see the incredible difference that God can make in their lives.

Early in 2011, our family made the momentous decision to leave Canberra and move thousands of kilometres away, to the far north of Australia. We planned to live in Darwin, a remote city with a tropical climate and a reputation for its spirit of independence. We love talking with people about God and, having spent years doing this in Canberra, we had decided to start a new church in a new location.

It was difficult to announce to our church in Canberra that we were moving on, but the time seemed right. We made preparations and encouraged some others to join with us in this new venture. After a couple of trips north we'd found a house, schools for our children, a job for my wife as a doctor at the local Aboriginal Health Service, a rugby club to join, and a boat ramp to launch the boat we were planning to buy. Although we'd never said so, I think both Fiona and I saw this as a mid-life move. We were looking forward to another twenty years in ministry in the Northern Territory.

The months leading up to our move were hectic. One of the other pastors at our church had been overseas for four months, so my workload was particularly heavy. In addition, since I was leaving, I'd accepted a number of invitations to speak at conferences. Although our plan was to leave in January, we packed up our house in late November to avoid the massive increase in moving costs over the Christmas period and were basically camping in our house. In the last week of November I spoke at a conference in Melbourne for people who were thinking about starting new churches. It was exciting to meet so many men and women heading out to new adventures. I was something of a poster boy—the middle-aged bloke who, instead of hanging up his boots, was venturing out for another season.

And I was ready to go—but for one baffling problem. Every time I'd climb the three flights of stairs to the conference dining room, I'd arrive at the top breathless. I'd slump over, gasping for air. I remember thinking that I was embarrassingly unfit. Too much coffee, too much food, not enough sleep, not enough exercise. But I knew all that would change instantly when we arrived in Darwin. I'd become the great outdoorsman—fishing, shooting, boating, four-wheel driving.

But on a Friday morning in early December I was so exhausted that I told my wife I thought something was wrong. I was feeling breathless and had numbness around my mouth. I described the pain between my shoulder blades and in my chest and neck. Fiona asked me a bunch of diagnostic questions and gave me a long hug. I discovered later that she was listening carefully to my chest and heart and beginning to suspect that maybe everything *wasn't* okay.

My swan song in Canberra was the opening talk at a university student ministry conference. Not only was I leaving Canberra and our church, I was also moving away from the university work that I'd been involved in as a student and pastor for so much of my life. Part of my tradition at this annual conference is meeting at a local coffee shop with a bunch of guys I've known for more than twenty years. I call us the 'old farts' of the student ministry movement. When we gather, each person shares what's been going on over the past year and then one or two of us pray for that person, and so on. These times of listening, sharing, and prayer have always been a tremendous encouragement to me. That year, though, I sat at that coffee shop wondering why everyone was taking forever. Why were they talking so slowly and for such a long time?

Why were their prayers so tedious and drawn out? It's not that I was waiting for my turn to come around; it was that the numbness in my arms and legs was getting worse by the minute. There was something wrong, and I needed to tell someone. I finally interrupted the prayer. It was difficult to get the words out.

One of my friends in the group had trained as a doctor, and he took charge immediately. We headed straight to emergency at the local hospital. He instructed the others to go directly to the counter and say, "Query heart attack." (I tell you, if you're ever waiting for hours in emergency, hoping to catch the attention of the nurses, just say, "Query heart attack." You get the royal treatment. No waiting. Straight into a wheelchair, through the doors, into a bed, and hooked up to an ECG machine. No forms to fill in or questions asked.)

I didn't feel well, but I knew I was in the right place. Someone phoned Fiona. Someone else went to pick up my car. A couple of the guys hung around, waiting for information. Someone called the conference organizers and fifteen hundred students began to pray for me.

The ECG seemed normal. I wasn't having a heart attack. I thought it was probably just an arrhythmia. I'd had them before, so I knew I'd be back to normal in no time. But the doctors kept asking me questions. The pain between my shoulders had them worried. They were still thinking 'heart', and apparently this kind of pain is a regular symptom of an aortic rupture. I went for an X-ray, which showed nothing. So they wheeled me off for a CT scan.

By the time Fiona arrived, everyone was baffled. They knew something was wrong, but they didn't know what it was until they examined the scan. The CT showed a huge build-up of fluid around my left lung, in the pleural cavity. There was a dark patch on the edge of the lung.

The senior doctor spoke. "We think you could have a tumour," she said. My throat contracted and I felt sick to my stomach. The tear ducts opened and disbelief overwhelmed me. This couldn't happen to me, to my family. I felt as though some judge had just sentenced me to death.

Why? How? What? My questions tumbled over one another.

"It could be a mesothelioma, the asbestos disease," the doctor said.

But that didn't make sense. I couldn't remember ever being exposed. Although I wasn't positive that our house was free of asbestos, I certainly hadn't disturbed it. I'd done some caving, climbing through piles of bat poo. Could that have caused this?

"It could be a lung cancer," she said.

But that didn't make sense either. I wasn't a smoker. Although I'd tried it as a teenager, and the school bus was always full of smoke and I hung around others who smoked, it wasn't enough to cause lung cancer. We had to wait until they could get inside to take a look and know for sure.

In the meantime, they needed to drain the fluid. This procedure brought on the first of a number of attempts I made to pass out. The needle had to go between my ribs, and it kept getting stuck. Every time they came to a dead end, I did my best to collapse, unconscious. Eventually the radiologist succeeded, with the help of a guided ultrasound, and he extracted two litres of fluid from the pleural cavity around my lungs. Two litres of fluid were pressing on my lungs—no wonder I was breathless. And there was more to come.

We had to make some major decisions that weekend. Our furniture and belongings were somewhere en route between Canberra and Darwin. Would we follow after them? Or did we need to have the moving company turn around and bring everything back to Canberra? The medical advice seemed clear. Whatever was wrong wasn't going to be resolved quickly, so it didn't seem wise to leave for the remote far north of Australia. It made sense to stay with family, friends, church, and a medical system we understood. Perhaps, we reasoned, we'd be able to move to Darwin once I got better, but for the time being we had to stay. We held a family conference in the hospital with all four children. It was devastating.

"We're pretty sure dad has a lung cancer. No, we're not going to be able to go to Darwin. No, we don't know how bad it is, but it doesn't look good."

It all seemed so unreal. And so unfair.

The doctors let me go home the next day to spend time with my family and celebrate our twenty-eighth wedding anniversary. This wasn't exactly what I had planned. I don't remember what I did have planned, but I'm sure it didn't involve wearing a hospital admissions bracelet.

Surgery that Monday confirmed that I had a primary lung cancer. A tumour on the outside of the left lung had ruptured, and the cancer had spread to the pleural lining. This was not good news. There are medical options for those who catch lung cancer before it spreads, because sometimes doctors can remove a lobe or even a lung.

But the fact that the cancer had spread to other places put me into the serious category. The surgeon performed an operation to prevent the further build-up of fluid and inserted a tube into my chest to drain the remaining fluid.

When I returned to the ward I wasn't sure which of the specialists was my primary physician. A surgeon visited me to discuss the operation. A respiratory physician checked out my breathing. A pain specialist kept prescribing me drugs. And the oncologist turned up a few days later. He was the one I really wanted to see. I wanted answers. I wanted to know what was going on and how long it would take to get well.

But the oncologist was the one who uttered the second hopeless word. "It's incurable," he said. "We can't remove it."

I felt my throat contracting again. The tears started. My words were cracked and broken. I didn't understand. It was even more difficult because I heard this news without Fiona there. Why was he so pessimistic, so defeatist? He explained that because the cancer had spread, surgery wasn't an option. I asked about chemotherapy, and he told me that this type of cancer doesn't disappear with chemo. All he could offer was the possibility of helping me live a little longer.

I asked for the prognosis.

"You'll probably see next Christmas," he said.

Probably? What did he mean, 'probably'? He explained that I had stage-4 lung cancer, and that I might have another ten to thirteen months to live. The mortality rate for lung cancer is the highest among all the more common cancers. Very few people survive long after the cancer has spread.

In that moment, he drained my hope further. I felt the darkness of despair descending on me. I was alone. I was dying. I was stupid. I asked the dumb questions and I wasn't prepared for the answers. How could this be? Less than a week ago, I had been brimming with hope and excitement.

Within days the news went from bad, to very bad, to extremely bad. I deteriorated rapidly. The first operation wasn't successful, so they transferred me to a hospital that was better equipped. The doctors had to insert two new drains between my ribs into the pleural cavity. The pain-killing drugs gave me some frightening hallucinations. My constipation was so extreme that I had to vomit to remove food. I became so weak that I could barely move myself around in bed. I lost fifteen kilograms in three weeks. The emergency team was called twice as I plunged into unconsciousness. I experienced a 'ten out of ten' for pain when the nurse pulled out the second chest tube. I began to think that I was going to die in hospital.

Others suspected the same. Although I have memories of only a few, many people came to visit me. I imagine that some of them thought they were paying their final respects. We arranged for a lawyer to draw up my will. I signed over power of attorney to Fiona. We called in an accountant to explain our finances. I had chats with some of my kids about life without their dad. I shed many tears. My cancer was incurable. I was hopeless.

2 SHATTERED DREAMS

After my second operation, things began to improve. The nurses were more careful when removing my drainage tubes and the resulting pain was only seven out of ten. My strength began to return, enough for me to be able to walk the length of the ward while holding onto the rails. I was grateful for these signs of recovery, but I'd had enough of hospital and yearned to be home with my family. To my delight, the doctors released me in time for Christmas.

I returned home to a 'new' house. Fiona had arranged for new carpet and a hospital bed in the study—my makeshift hospital room—while Fiona remained in our bedroom. I couldn't have coped with someone else in the room and I had too much pain and discomfort to lie flat in bed. There weren't enough pillows in the world to make me comfortable, and I all but forgot what it was like to sleep through the night, waking regularly as I did in pain or needing to visit the toilet.

I made an effort to go to church on Christmas Day. Fiona said it would encourage people to see me there and she'd felt very alone without me on the previous two Sundays. We took a special chair for me to sit in and I didn't move from it. People came to me, but I couldn't talk with them. I didn't have the energy. In less than a month I'd become an invalid.

Kind and thoughtful friends prepared us exactly the kind of feast we'd have made for ourselves. Our whole family enjoyed a long lunch together in the backyard. It was such a relief to be home, to have the whole family together again. But uncertainty and fear cast shadows over our time together. Was the oncologist's prognosis correct? Would this be my last Christmas?

Although our family tradition had always been to enjoy holidays camping at the beach or visiting relatives over the summer months, I needed to convalesce at home. On the warmer days I'd sometimes sit in the backyard under the shade of the hazelnut trees. I enjoyed getting some sun and breathing in fresh air. I had to keep breathing, correctly and deeply, because my lungs needed some serious expanding. One time I sat and listened as the neighbours played badminton over the fence. They laughed and joked and teased. I started to cry. In fact, I sobbed. I couldn't play badminton, or basketball, or do anything active. I felt like an anchor slowing everyone down.

After months of excitement and making plans, two words—*tumour* and *incurable*—had shattered our dreams. We wouldn't move to Darwin, or participate in the birth of a new church, or live in the house we'd bought, or make new friends in a new neighbourhood, or explore new places, or spend Saturdays in the boat together. Cancer had taken all of that away from us.

As I rested and reflected that summer, I began to see more clearly how I had been looking forward to this move as a second chance. It would have been an opportunity to start over again in ministry, from the beginning, but with the wisdom gained from more than twenty years of experience. I would have been able to implement what I'd learned from my mistakes, apply new ideas, and try new strategies with a different group of people in a different community with a different vibe. Fiona and I had been looking forward to reconnecting and planning, dreaming, praying, and doing more together as a couple. The children were keen to contribute. This was going to be a family enterprise. It sounds idyllic, and no doubt we were idealistic, but this was the dream that those two words had shattered.

Yet, painful as all this was, it wasn't the dashing of these hopes that hurt the most. Grief for my family and for what I might never experience overwhelmed me. I didn't want to leave my wife a widow with all the responsibility for raising our family. I didn't want to leave my children without a father. How would they deal with this kind of loss? I might never hold any of my grandchildren. I might not walk my daughter down the aisle. I might miss my son's graduation. Who would my kids marry? I might not meet their life partners. What if they got together with the wrong people? How would their lives turn out? I hated the thought that I might not be there for them.

And so, gradually, my dreams were replaced by despair. The negatives loomed larger than the positives. I ached inside and I wept often, deeply, and uncontrollably. I wasn't ready to face my own mortality. Not yet. I wanted to wake up and pinch myself. Surely, I found myself thinking, this was only a dream—a nightmare. I just wanted it to go away. A friend had loaned us the British DVD series

Life on Mars. The lead character in the show has a serious accident, ends up in a coma, and lives a parallel life as a policeman thirty years earlier. It's hard to know what's real and what's not, and as I watched I kept waiting for him to wake up and return to reality. Our lives felt like *Life on Mars*. "Please, God," I prayed, "bring me out of this coma!"

But my cancer journey had only just begun. The doctors couldn't start the chemotherapy until I had recovered from surgery. They warned me that this treatment would be very harsh, so I needed to be fitter to cope. My frailty unnerved me. I'd always been reasonably fit, but at that point the only exercise I could manage was a slow shuffle up and down our street. I could barely lift my feet. Sometimes I tripped over cracks or garden edging, and it took me forever to walk one block. When my friends talked about swimming or surfing, mountain biking or running, going to the gym or hiking through national parks, my heart would sink. "I'll probably never do any of that again", I thought. I was doomed to be an invalid until the end.

It's not that I'd never been sick before. I'd had mumps and chicken pox and tonsillitis as a child. I'd undergone an embarrassing hernia operation when I was young. I'd suffered from recurring migraines as a teenager. I'd somehow managed to come down with the flu most winters. I'd struggled with bouts of vertigo that left me dizzy and disturbed. I'd broken a few bones playing sport and falling off bikes. I knew what it was to be incapacitated through illness or injury. But this was different. Before, I always knew I'd get better. But this was incurable.

Nearly two months after my diagnosis, after still more scans and tests, I began chemotherapy. We discussed options and decided on the most effective cocktail of drugs with the least damaging side effects. The downside was that we'd have to pay for the drugs ourselves. Not all of the drugs were government approved, and the insurance companies didn't provide coverage. The oncologist warned us that this could cost a huge amount of money. He couldn't say exactly how much, because it depended how long I lived. It would be thousands of dollars for each visit every three weeks. The longer I lived, the more it would cost. If I responded well, the total cost could rise into hundreds of thousands of dollars. What a choice. As I left the hospital after that consultation, I wondered what the point was. In my despair I told Fiona that I might as well give up now and save my family the money. She told me not to be so depressingly stupid.

"At least you've got your health", people often say when things go wrong. But I didn't. I had a wife, children, friends, family, and a church. They loved me and supported me. But the fear of dying and leaving them all behind was crushing.

People say that it's common to fall into depression when you get cancer—not necessarily a chemical depression, but the melancholy that accompanies deep loss. I began to feel something like this taking over my life. I lacked motivation and desire. I cried easily and saw myself changing, which worried me all the more. I became anxious about my anxiety. I feared slipping into serious depression. People tried to comfort me. Some said everything was going to be all right. Some even told me they *knew* that I was going to be healed. But their words seemed empty. They were loving and well motivated but powerless to effect the changes I needed.

The frailty of my body affected my mind. Weakness and weariness replaced drive and motivation. It was hard to be optimistic when I ached all over. It was difficult to think clearly when I was doped up with painkillers. The doctors told me to expect that this would be the new normal.

Chemotherapy is brutal. One doctor described it as figuring out the dose of poison that would kill the patient and then dialling it back a notch. Others liken it to weedkiller or rat poison. This poison attacks the fastest-growing cells in the body. This includes cancer cells, but it also includes the guts, the gums, the tongue, the stomach, the intestinal linings, the sexual organs, the hair, the palms, the soles of the feet, and more. The chemo made me feel like I had an extreme case of the flu—the classic 'being hit by a truck' feeling. There are intense short-term side effects and potentially serious long-term consequences.

In many ways I still had no idea what lay ahead. I knew people who'd had cancer. I'd visited people at their bedsides and watched them waste away. I'd witnessed the brutality of the treatments. I'd prayed with people and seen some recover, but I'd seen others die. I'd lost friends and relatives to this cruel and indiscriminate disease. I'd conducted funerals and wept with those who mourned. I thought I knew something of cancer, but I couldn't appreciate the multiple layers of pain and loss it creates until I began to experience these things myself.

Cancer took so much away from us and threatened to take still more—my vitality, the future we'd planned but would never experience, the dreams that were no longer realistic, my life. Where, I wondered in the midst of all this loss and fear, could I ever find hope?

3 SEARCHING FOR HOPE

What is hope? Is it an emotion or a feeling? Or is hope a way of thinking? Is hope simply a reaction to our circumstances? Or can we develop hope and train our minds to be hopeful?

Hope is a function of both thinking and feeling. Hopeful feelings arise from hopeful thoughts. And if we're feeling hopeful we're more disposed to searching and finding reasons for hope. It also works the other way. When we can't think of any reasons for hope we become prone to despair. And despair can cloud our thinking and blind us to good reasons for hope.

Whether we're talking about feelings or thoughts, though, hope always has to do with a *positive future orientation*. It requires that we see beyond current circumstances to a time when things will be better. This could also be a definition for wishful thinking, of course, so we need to measure the quality of hope by the strength of the reasons that lie behind it. Real hope requires solid reasons for thinking and feeling positively about an improved future. Weak or false hope may be nothing more than irrational optimism.

Hope matters. Without hope there's nothing to live for. It's been said that "Where there's life there is hope", but it's equally important to say that "Where there's hope there is life". Hope is related to quality as well as quantity of life. I suspect that much of the push for euthanasia comes from a desire to avoid a hopeless quality of life. People question the point of living when they feel despair. It's easy to criticize this view of the world but, when you're the subject of two words like *tumour* and *incurable*, questions of life and death take on a new and personal significance. Although I never seriously considered taking my own life, I certainly resonated with the questions people ask about the point of living.

I couldn't make sense of anything in those first weeks and months. I didn't understand what was happening to me and I had little idea where I could turn for help. Above all, however, I struggled to find hope.

The obvious question facing me was this: "Do I have any good reasons for thinking positively about a better future?" When my life expectancy dropped from years to months, when the days ahead offered little but pain and weakness and decline, when my dreams were destroyed, when all I could feel was loss… did I have any good reasons for hope? I began to search and, bit by bit, reasons emerged.

Hope in medicine

Although I was present at the births of each of our four children, had visited our fragile premature daughter in hospital every day for months, and had often been to see others in hospital over the years, I had always prided myself in my ability to avoid hospitals. I'm happy to visit as long as I don't have to stay.

The thing I like least about hospitals is… well, that they're full of sick people. Someone is always groaning or coughing, being bandaged or x-rayed. The patients look like prisoners, dressed in ridiculous white smocks that show off their undies. Some are attached to tubes and monitors. Some have blood going in and fluids coming out. Some are diseased and fragile and old and dying. To be honest, I don't like hospitals because they remind me of death.

I went into hospital in December 2011 believing I was reasonably healthy, and came out knowing I wasn't. Just weeks earlier I'd been lifting furniture and packing my house, and then all of a sudden I could barely lift my feet or walk to the bathroom. I weighed 93kg on the way in and 78kg on the way out. All in three weeks—not a bad weight loss regime, but I don't think I could sell it! So, I ask, where is the hope in hospitals?

I wouldn't be sitting here, writing this book, if it weren't for modern medicine and the training, experience, equipment and resources of medical specialists. I've had x-rays, blood tests, biopsies, and CT, PET and bone scans. Accurate diagnosis has given me hope for better treatment—not absolute hope of a cure, but hope nonetheless.

Now, after more than a year and a half of chemotherapy, my health is better than I could have imagined. I've enjoyed gradual improvements and feel much more hopeful than I did at the start. I think my mind is better, too—though that could just be the chemo playing tricks on me! I've been forced to learn patience and humility, even though I still have a long way to go. I've lived longer than was expected, and this has opened all kinds of new opportunities for me. Not in a million years could I have imagined that would involve writing a blog, or a book, not to mention helping others who have cancer.

I've learned that cancer is not one-size-fits-all. It's a range of possible problems with a corresponding range of potential treatments. Accurate diagnosis, thorough testing, second opinions—they're all important. Not everyone responds to treatment in the same way. My father responded brilliantly to chemotherapy for his cancer, which is different from mine. After six treatments there was no evidence of disease in his body. As I write this, I've had twenty-six three-weekly cycles of chemo, and my cancer is still present. There's so much we just don't know.

While medicine offers some hope, it has its limitations and there are no guarantees. Medical intervention has improved my quality of life, but it has also made it worse. The side effects of chemo are horrendous. I've been told not to expect a cure, and yet I continue to pray that it will happen. I have good reasons to place hope in medicine—but not all my hope, and not my ultimate hope. For I know that even if I am cured of cancer, one day I will die of something else.

My ongoing challenge is to keep my hope focused on God. God can cure me if he so chooses—whether by medicine or miracle. He oversees all things, including medical science, to bring about his good purposes. Medicine is one of God's generous gifts to offer us hope, but it's only hope for this life. Hope that endures in the face of death will not be found in medical science.

Hope in lifestyle

I have no control over my cancer, but I can choose how I live with cancer. I can choose, each day, to live in hope. And that involves making some very practical, positive choices.

For example, exercise helps. I'm not as fit as I was, but then I never have been! In hospital my main exercise was breathing—deliberately and deeply. Now walking is the most I can usually manage, and my body and mind benefit when I do it. I can eat sensibly, sleep regularly, rest, get out when I can, and go with the flow when I can't. These are not profound choices that lead me to the meaning of life, but they are simple ways to help me make more of life.

It's tough living 24/7 in the land of cancer. I love those times when I'm able to forget that I even have cancer—when I play a game of Scrabble with friends, cheer on my favourite rugby team, catch fish with the kids, spend time away with the family, do what 'normal' people do. It has helped me to realize that cancer doesn't need to define me or shape my every moment. And laughter is good medicine. Watching comedies, spending time with funny people, listening to jokes, and rediscovering some of the things that once brought me joy all help. I've never much been one for crying, but cancer has changed that. It's an excellent pressure release valve.

Clarifying priorities, focusing on what matters, and deciding to live every day with purpose help me to remain hopeful. All of our lifestyle choices make a difference, but they can never deliver real hope. One day—and it could be sooner rather than later—all of those choices will disappear.

Hope in relationships

Good relationships also have a big impact on our mental and physical wellbeing. Unresolved conflict, tension, bitterness, jealousy, and anger can all hurt us more than we realize. Loving and supporting relationships can help to keep us, and those close to us, healthy and hope-filled.

As I face my cancer, so do my family and friends. My wife has provided me with constant encouragement, support, and love since my diagnosis. I know it's a cliché, but I absolutely don't know what I would have done without her. Fiona has been my deepest friend, carer, lover, intercessor, advocate, nurse, doctor, organizer, personal trainer, empathizer, researcher, challenger, confronter, communicator, caring mother to our children, and much more. We have our share of ups and downs. We're not strangers to conflict. Yet as we work through these things together, they strengthen our relationship and our hope of things to come. And so in turn we share this hope with our children and with extended family and friends.

Relationships have played a big part in my healing over recent months. I still have cancer, but I am a different person in many ways. I no longer take life, love, family, or friendships for granted. Each relationship is precious and brings me hope. But everyone I love will, one day, be taken away.

Hope in understanding

I've learned a lot since I was first diagnosed with cancer. I've learned from my doctors, from books and articles and blogs, and from forums that put me in touch with others who understand. It's sometimes been a challenge to get the best, most accurate and relevant information, but over time my hope has grown as understanding has replaced my ignorance and fears.

At first I believed cancer was an automatic death sentence. I lost hope because I knew so little. I assumed that the words of the oncologist were fact—thirteen months was all I could expect. Now I understand that his prognosis was a calculated guess, based on knowledge and experience. But knowledge and experience are growing all the time and new treatments and options are being developed and discovered at a rapid rate.

So far my circumstances have been changing for the better, but what if I get sicker and the cancer spreads and death draws closer? Can knowledge and understanding offer me hope when the prognosis is not optimistic? Won't understanding simply help me to be clearer about how hopeless things are?

My cancer diagnosis has brought me to a deeper understanding of my own mortality. When I believed cancer was a death sentence I was wrong—not because I'm not going to die, but because in fact I'd always lived under the shadow of death. The one thing we know for sure is that we're going to die. Increased understanding can only give me deep and lasting hope, then, if it points me to a way to overcome death.

Limited and false hope

While medicine, healthy choices, relationships, and increased understanding all give us some measure of hope, none of these things can sustain the full burden of hope or give us the kind of hope that endures in the face of death. But these little day-by-day hopes, limited as they are, are all worth celebrating. If we require nothing less than a complete cure in order to find hope then we will miss out on a lot.

The word of caution, however, is that false hope can cause us to miss the real thing. People are prone to clutching at anything that promises hope. Dating sites claim that finding the perfect partner is the key to intimacy and pleasure. Organizations claim that working for them will offer security and satisfaction. Superannuation companies claim that the secret to hope and happiness is a strong retirement plan. All of these claims tend to promise more than they can deliver, and those who seek hope in them are inevitably disappointed.

For those with terminal illness who are desperately seeking a cure—or anything that might prolong life—false hopes are on offer everywhere. Typing 'cancer cures' into Google brings up links to fourteen million different sites. How do I work out what to do with that? In all of these things, we need to be discerning. Some offer completely false, even dangerous, hope. Others will indeed offer limited hope. But brokenness, pain, suffering, and death are realities of life in this world. No amount of education or money, no career, health or human relationship can protect us from our mortality. So then what? Is there still hope?

The good versus the best

A friend of mine loves reminding people, "Don't let the good become the enemy of the best". We have looked at many *good* reasons for hope, but they are not the *best* reasons for hope because each of these things will one day come to an end. Death is certain, and it's the great enemy of hope. If I put my hope only in things that will one day be destroyed or taken from me, then—regardless of how good they might be for a time—I will miss out on the greatest source of hope available.

I'm persuaded that there is a source of hope that is above and beyond any hope this world can offer. The source of this hope is God himself. Some will complain that this is wishful thinking or dismiss it as a crutch. Others will consider it naïve and say that it avoids the real issues. Still others might think that introducing God is a distraction and beside the point. If you are entertaining any of these thoughts as you read this, I encourage you to hold on to the question that brought you to this book in the first place as you read on and consider: What if this hope that cannot be destroyed by anything in this world of pain and disappointment is real? What then?

This hope is firmly anchored in history. It's not the subject of myths and legends but of verifiable events and public evidence. It's found in history departments, alongside the writings of Philo and Josephus—not on the fantasy fiction shelves with *Harry Potter* and *The Hobbit*. This hope is anchored in the reality that Jesus Christ was crucified, buried in a tomb, and then resurrected from the dead.

This hope is based on faith. It's not a blind leap in the dark but a logical, reasonable, intelligent faith based on the testimonies of many eyewitnesses. But this faith runs far deeper than an intellectual belief in an ideology or philosophy. This faith involves placing my life and death in the hands of God, who sacrificed his own Son to give me this real, solid hope. It means trusting in Jesus Christ, and his death and resurrection, for the forgiveness of my sins. It means relying on Jesus to bring me through the horrors of death and into eternity with God.

Faith and reason have shaped this book. Together they have given me hope. I don't know everything there is to know about cancer or God. I've studied them both, but my understanding is partial and limited. My ignorance outweighs my knowledge, even though I'm learning more day by day. But this knowledge of cancer and of God isn't simply in my head—it's deeply personal. I don't just know *about* them—they are part of my *life* and my *experience*. I know cancer and I know God. And it's because I know God that I believe there is real hope for those who have cancer, for those who are struggling, for those who have lost hope—for everyone.

4 FAITH

Cancer stole my future and threatened to steal my hope. It's an ugly killer, and I hate it, but it has pushed me to refocus on the things that matter. Cancer has been my reality check, reminding me that one day I will die—and it might well be sooner than I'd planned. Death is always a rude affront to life. It breaks up families, destroys friendships, and makes a mockery of many of our aspirations.

Cancer is certainly not always a death sentence. Many people overcome their disease and continue to live in good health for many years. My grandfather was diagnosed with cancer in his fifties, received effective treatment, and lived into his nineties. I'm hoping and praying for a similar story. Nonetheless, a cancer diagnosis is always a serious matter. A serious illness reminds us of our frailty and vulnerability and makes the fact that we will all die more real.

The society I live in covers up death and hides it away. I was in my twenties before I saw a dead body. When I was studying social work at university, one of my classes took a trip to the Sydney morgue. We were invited to look at a body on a television monitor. If we were okay with this, then we could enter a room to view a corpse from behind the glass. The next step was to enter another room with bodies laid out on tables. Grey, lifeless bodies of men and women we knew nothing about. The memory of that experience still sends chills up my spine.

Although it might seem strange to keep coming back to death in a book about hope, we've seen that real hope must be able to offer something substantial in the face of death. Hope that avoids the truth of our mortality is limited, temporary, and ultimately impotent.

Few of us have any clue about when we're going to die. We expect we'll live as long as most other people. Seventy, eighty, even ninety years seems reasonable these days. We look at our parents or grandparents and assume we'll enjoy a similar life span. If this is still many years off, then it's easy to delay thinking about what happens when we die. Consequently, we get very practised at putting off any thoughts about death and dying, let alone what might happen after death.

Being diagnosed with cancer or another serious illness can be a timely warning to get one's life in order. It certainly was for me, and I'm not talking about organizing powers of attorney, updating a will or planning a funeral—I'm talking about getting things right with God. My diagnosis, and the fears and doubts that followed, pushed me to go back to the core beliefs of Christianity.

Doubts and belief

Facing the reality of my own mortality put my beliefs to the test. Is there really a God? Do I trust him? Can I face death without fear of what lies beyond? Is there life after death?

Can I be sure of going to be with God when I die? What about judgement? Will God accept me? My experience of having cancer amplified all my questions and doubts.

I grew up in a Christian family with Christian parents and Christian grandparents, and expressed faith in Jesus at a young age. One might say that I was born to believe— that I was simply a cultural Christian. But while I was at university, atheistic humanism competed with my thoughts about God. My world was in conflict and I had to work out what I believed. So I read books and bothered people constantly with my questions. I discovered that, though I had called myself a Christian, I wasn't entirely clear what a Christian was. I wondered if I had to be good enough for God to accept me. I knew, deep down, that I didn't even live up to my own expectations. I wondered if I needed to remember every bad thing I'd ever done and ask forgiveness for each one. I knew I'd never be able to do that. And I wondered how Jesus fit into things.

I don't know exactly when it happened, but things gradually clicked into place for me. I found answers to most of my questions and became persuaded that the Christian message was true. I understood that Christianity was great news and offered great hope. Even though I had failed God and would continue to do so, God was willing to accept me because of Jesus.

Here's a short summary of what I came to believe— Christianity in four points:

1. *God* created this wonderfully vast and intricate universe. And he created us to enjoy a relationship with him in which we honour him by trusting his word.

2. *We* prefer independence from God, refuse to trust him, and live our own way. This is called sin. God

promises to bring judgement on us for turning against him.

3. *God* never gives up on us. He showed his deep love for us when he sent Jesus to take the judgement for our sin by dying on a cross. God raised Jesus to life and calls people to trust Jesus and turn back to him.

4. *We* can be right with God if we confess our sin, trust in Jesus' death in our place, and honour Jesus as our God. If we continue to reject God, then we will face his judgement without hope.

As a pastor, I've spent many years reading, studying and teaching these things. I've encouraged people to believe the Bible, to have confidence in God's promises, to pray and put their faith in Jesus Christ. I've sat with the sick and dying, prayed with them, and comforted them with the hope of life beyond death. But my diagnosis brought me face to face with fears and doubts that were very personal, scary and raw.

I'd grown comfortable with my faith over the years, and my cancer diagnosis began to seriously test that faith. Everything became more important and urgent. I began questioning my convictions. Did I really believe? Was it true or had I been kidding myself? Were there good reasons to have faith? I found myself asking questions and searching for answers with an eagerness I hadn't experienced in years. In the weeks and months following my diagnosis, I went back to the Bible to read things afresh. I asked questions, watched interviews with experts, and read books about the reasons for Christian belief.

Reading the Bible provided competition for my doubts and fears. When I ignored God, my fears and uncertainty grew. When I read the Bible, listening to God speak, he provided answers and strengthened my faith. It was a battle. Staying neutral on these questions was not an option. A complacent faith might feel comfortable, but it isn't really a faith at all. And when cancer invaded my body and my prognosis set the clock ticking, I became very uncomfortable. Either there is a God and he's worth listening to—or there's no God and it's all up to me. I needed to be sure.

Looking to Jesus

My investigations brought me back to the central truth that Jesus is the key to faith in God. The evidence for Jesus Christ is very strong—no serious historian disputes his existence. Jesus made claims to be God, and his words, life, and miracles backed up his claims. He offered help and hope to people who were downtrodden and suffering. He healed the sick and raised the dead. Jesus invited the weary and burdened to find rest for their souls by coming to him. He offered the way and the means to know God and to be known by God.

As I read more and more about Jesus in the months following my diagnosis I found my faith growing. I began to feel a peace and confidence in trusting Jesus that I knew I would never find anywhere else. Even if doctors were able to offer me a complete cure, it would only be temporary. Jesus offered me something far deeper and more enduring. As I read through the gospels—the four books in the New Testament by Matthew, Mark, Luke, and John that give us eyewitness accounts of Jesus' life—I began to see a pattern. While Jesus often cured people, relieving them of their physical sickness and symptoms, he also kept pointing them to a deeper hope that addressed their deeper problems. What he was offering them was a *hope beyond cure*.

We see Jesus doing this when some men bring their friend, who is paralyzed, to him to be healed. Instead of simply healing his legs, Jesus addresses the problems in his heart and soul:

> Some men came, bringing to him a paralyzed man, carried by four of them. Since they could not get him to Jesus because of the crowd, they made an opening in the roof above Jesus by digging through it and then lowered the mat the man was lying on. When Jesus saw their faith, he said to the paralyzed man, "Son, your sins are forgiven".
>
> Now some teachers of the law were sitting there, thinking to themselves, "Why does this fellow talk like that? He's blaspheming! Who can forgive sins but God alone?"
>
> Immediately Jesus knew in his spirit that this was what they were thinking in their hearts, and he said to them, "Why are you thinking these things? Which is easier: to say to this paralyzed man, 'Your sins are forgiven,' or to say, 'Get up, take your mat and walk'? But I want you to know that the Son of Man has authority on earth to forgive sins." So he said to the man, "I tell you, get up, take your mat and go home". He got up, took his mat and walked out in full view of them all. This amazed everyone and they praised God, saying, "We have never seen anything like this!" (Mark chapter 2, verses 3-12)

I assume that the forgiveness of this man's sins was the last thing his four friends had on their minds. They had either seen Jesus healing serious illnesses and disabilities or heard about his ability to do so, so they did all they could to make sure their friend got a piece of the action. They must have been dismayed when all Jesus did was forgive his sins—what a letdown! But Jesus had given him something far better. Forgiveness is the only gateway to deep healing that lasts forever. One action—healing the paralysis—lasted only a few years, until he died. The other—forgiveness—lasted beyond death for eternity.

Diagnosing our deepest problem

We don't have to look far to find clear evidence that there are deep problems with our world. Cancer and death are but two pieces of that evidence. We might be tempted to blame God for the mess, but it's not his fault. The first chapter of the first book of the Bible, Genesis 1, tells us that God created the world and everything in it and it was "good". Genesis 1 also tells us that God created human beings "in his own image". Although the image of God is a complex concept, it's clear that God created us out of his love and desire to be in relationship with us. But all of us choose to push God away. We don't trust that God, the all-powerful creator, knows what's right or best. We think that if we make our own decisions independently from God then our lives and our world will be all the better for it.

Since people have responded to God this way since the very beginning, it's worth asking whether we've succeeded in making our world a better place. Are we better off with God or without him? An unbiased look at our world, and an honest assessment of our thoughts and behaviours, will tell us that we're not doing so well by pushing God away.

Blood tests, ultrasounds, and CT scans will never reveal my deepest problem—but the Bible does. God diagnoses my deepest problem, and it's not cancer—it's sin. I choose to ignore God and live by my own standards and rules. We all do it. We replace God with things that aren't God, and we live for these things instead. We might decide that our reputation, or home, or family, or career, or health, or investments, or any number of other things is what's most important to us. As a result, we end up living for 'stuff' rather than for God. We worship things that God has made rather than God himself. It's pretty crass, really. If I loved someone and gave them everything they needed, and then they ignored me and lived as though I didn't exist, I would be devastated. But that's how we treat God. The Bible puts it in these terms:

> The wrath of God is being revealed from heaven against all the godlessness and wickedness of people, who suppress the truth by their wickedness, since what may be known about God is plain to them, because God has made it plain to them. For since the creation of the world God's invisible qualities— his eternal power and divine nature—have been clearly seen, being understood from what has been made, so that people are without excuse.
>
> For although they knew God, they neither glorified him as God nor gave thanks to him, but their thinking became futile and their foolish hearts were darkened. Although they claimed to be wise, they became fools and exchanged the glory of the

immortal God for images made to look like a mortal human being and birds and animals and reptiles. (Romans chapter 1, verses 18-23)[1]

God has made himself known. The planets and stars, the mountains and seas, the delicate flowers, the intricacies of the human body—they all testify to God's greatness. We marvel at the creation, but often we ignore the one who created it. This is our deepest problem—rather than thanking God, we tell him to mind his own business. It's no wonder that God isn't happy with us.

God's response to our deliberate rejection is to bring death and decay into our world. Sickness, cancer, and death are all part of his judgement. From the moment we're born we live under the shadow of death. We've forfeited the joy of living in harmony with God, and instead we experience the pain of fractured and broken relationships. Through our own selfishness we cause damage to ourselves, to other people and to our environment. Suffering, hurt, tragedy and grief have become a normal part of human experience. Cancer—my cancer, all cancers—is part of this messed up, decaying world. None of this explains why specific things happen to specific people, but it certainly puts them in context.

Faith in the death of Jesus

Even though it sometimes seems as though God is a long way off and uninterested in what we've been going

---

1 The apostle Paul's letter to the church in Rome, which is the book of Romans in the New Testament, directly addresses many of the questions we're considering in this chapter.

through, he hasn't forgotten us. It's in this depressing context of sickness and suffering and death that God offers hope. Death is not God's final statement. He promises that, if we put our trust in Jesus, we can look forward to a day when there will be no more sickness and death, when God will restore creation and people will enjoy the wonder of living in harmony with God and each other. As Romans chapter 8 says, "...the creation itself will be liberated from its bondage to decay and brought into the freedom and glory of the children of God" (verse 21). God offers us hope beyond death based on one unrepeatable, irreversible act of sacrifice: the death of Jesus.

We need to understand that Jesus' death was no ordinary death. I'm not talking about the circumstances of his death but about its significance. Jesus died on a wooden cross outside Jerusalem around two thousand years ago. The Bible and various other ancient historical documents record this event. These are the *circumstances* of his death. Yet Jesus died to pay the penalty for our rejection of God. He died as our representative and substitute to satisfy the judgement of God that we deserve. This is the *significance* of his death. This is the reason why Christians celebrate the day Jesus died as *Good* Friday. It's good because it offers us hope.

When I was struggling with my questions and doubts as a young man at university, two verses from the Bible clarified for me what a Christian was and how I could become one. These verses, again from Romans, focus on the death of Jesus Christ to explain how God has shown his love for us:

But God demonstrates his own love for us in this: While we were still sinners, Christ died for us.

> Since we have now been justified by his blood,
> how much more shall we be saved from God's wrath
> through him! (Romans chapter 5, verses 8-9)

God took the initiative. He didn't wait for me to reach out to him, change my ways and become a good religious person. It was while I was a "sinner" that God demonstrated his love. The proof of God's love is the death of Jesus Christ upon the cross. God sent his one and only Son, whom he loved, to die in my place. His death 'justifies' sinners—it delivers the verdict of 'not guilty'. This means that Jesus (the innocent one) has taken my sin and died for me (the guilty one) to pay the penalty for my judgement and satisfy God's justice. My faith is in Jesus' death, because he dealt with my sin on the cross.

We can find hope in the face of our own deaths by placing our faith in Jesus' death. Without Jesus we're headed for death and judgement, but with Jesus we can look forward to a hope-filled future in relationship with God. God promises to accept the death of Jesus as full payment for our sin. He will declare us not guilty and spare us from his judgement so that we can come before him knowing that we've been forgiven.

This truth offers enormous comfort. When I struggled with uncertainty about how God viewed me, my problem was that I was focused on myself. I believed it was up to me to make myself acceptable to God. It's liberating to know that being at peace with God has nothing to do with what I *do* for him. It's all about what he's already *done* for me in Jesus. All God asks of me is that I turn back to him and put my faith in Jesus.

Understanding faith

There seems to be a lot of confusion about the nature of faith, about what it is and isn't. Faith is not a religious feeling that some have and others don't. Faith is something we all exercise, every day, in many different contexts. We have faith in all sorts of things—in people's promises, in doctors, in Wikipedia, in motor vehicles, in the food we eat, even in the chairs we sit on. Faith is the exercise of trust or dependence in some thing or someone. What's important is not having faith but, rather, the object of that faith. Is there a good reason to have faith enough to get in that car? Well, it depends on whether the car is roadworthy and the driver is competent. Is it reasonable to trust doctors to look after your cancer? Again, it depends on what kind of doctors they are, on what knowledge and skills they possess, on whether they are sadistic murderers or compassionate healers.

Is there good reason for me to trust the death of Jesus? Yes—Jesus, the Son of God, died on the cross to take the judgement for my sin. God's faithfulness is more important than my faith. God promised to deal with the problem of our sin. He promised to clean our blemished records and give us hope beyond death. The death of Jesus is all about God keeping these promises. He can be trusted. We can place our faith in God. More than any friend, more than the expertise of any specialist, more than we can even trust ourselves—we can have faith in the promises of God.

As I looked back through my Bible, asking the hard questions and tackling my fears and doubts, I became more and more convinced that I could trust God in life *and* death. Every time I picked up the Bible I discovered promises that God had made—and I found that he had kept every one of them in Jesus Christ. As the apostle Paul wrote, "no matter how many promises God has made, they are 'Yes' in Christ" (2 Corinthians chapter 1, verse 20). Despite what my circumstances seem to be telling me, the death of Jesus changes everything because it is clear evidence that God loves me. All God asks of me is to trust him, to put my faith in the death of Jesus Christ.

God asks the same of us all. Will our hope, even in the face of death, be in Jesus Christ? Will we depend on the one who would rather die for us than give up on us? Will we put our faith in Jesus Christ, the one who has conquered death and who lives today?

5 HOPE

The doctors told me that I had no hope of being cured because my cancer was too advanced. *Tumour. Incurable.* I was devastated and hopeless. There were no medical options for removing the cancer; the best they could offer was to try to keep me alive longer by slowing the progression of the cancer. Since I had no hope of a cure, I had to look from the very beginning for hope beyond a cure.

That sounds ridiculous, doesn't it? *No hope of cure means death. Therefore, hope beyond cure means hope beyond death.* It's like saying, "If I can't find a cure for cancer then I want to find a way of coming back from the dead". Which is going to be easier? Surely, with all the resources and advances of scientists and medical professionals, it's statistically more likely that a cure will be found for my disease. They're discovering new things all the time. Lots of people beat cancer, even after doctors give them very little hope. But no-one beats the odds when it comes to death. If we're not going to die of cancer, it's guaranteed that we'll die of something else. Everyone dies—that's life.

So why would I be so naïve as to hope for a life beyond death? It is because God has promised eternal life to all who put their trust in Jesus Christ. Once again it comes back to the evidence. Can God be trusted? Is there anyone who can verify that God will raise people from the dead? Has it happened already? Can we find some supporting evidence or testimonies?

As I lay in my hospital bed, with terminal cancer and little hope of recovery, questions of life beyond death weighed upon me. Was Jesus really physically raised from the dead? How do we know? What if it's all a big hoax? It's one thing to live with a delusion, but I don't want to die putting all my hope in that delusion. The questions came thick and fast. They frightened me. I ached as I mulled over them. But I was determined to engage with them—to know for certain if my beliefs were real or whether I was simply deluding myself.

Again, I went back to the Bible to see if it held the answers to my questions. I revisited the reasons I first believed. I remembered how I had engaged with doubts in the past. It was a little scary to ask such brutally frank questions about my own death, but my diagnosis left me no time for soft-pedalling or procrastination. This was death and life stuff. There was no point pretending; I had to be sure.

Resurrection matters

Everything hinges on Jesus Christ. If God raised Jesus from the dead, then I know I can trust him. The resurrection validates Jesus' words and his actions, and gives substance to our hope of life beyond death.[2] If Jesus was not resurrected

2 I found the first letter that Paul wrote to the early Corinthian church (a book in the New Testament called 1 Corinthians) to be very helpful as I re-examined the evidence for, and implications of, the resurrection. We'll look at different verses from 1 Corinthians in this section as we think about why resurrection matters.

on that first Easter Sunday, then all who trust in Jesus are to be pitied because they're living with false hope. As Paul says in his first letter to the Corinthians:

> If only for this life we have hope in Christ, we are of all people most to be pitied. (1 Corinthians chapter 15, verse 19)

We can't have it both ways. It's either true or false; it's all or nothing. Some people like the idea of God and religion at a funeral. They like thinking about ending up in heaven or going to a better place. But when you're facing death, it doesn't matter what you like to hear or think about or what your personal preferences are. What matters is evidence.

When I was younger, one of my favourite movies was *Flatliners*, starring Kiefer Sutherland, Julia Roberts and Kevin Bacon. Sutherland's character persuades his fellow medical students to check out what lies beyond death. He 'flatlines' for one minute while his colleagues prepare to bring him back. Each of the students goes through this experience, putting their trust in the others to bring them back from death. The 'flatline' times get longer and the process of revival becomes more difficult and dangerous.

When I speak of hope beyond death, I'm not talking about a controlled 'flatline' experiment. Nor am I speaking of so-called 'near death' experiences with lights at the end of the tunnel. I'm referring to dead people coming back to life. If cancer destroys my vital organs and I'm pronounced dead, if there is a funeral and a cremation or burial, can I genuinely hope to be raised to life again? I'm putting this bluntly, I know, but terminal cancer doesn't allow much freedom for sentimentality.

The apostle Paul, who claimed to be a witness to the

resurrected Jesus, recognized the all-or-nothing significance of these events. He spells out some of the implications:

> And if Christ has not been raised, our preaching is useless and so is your faith. More than that, we are then found to be false witnesses about God, for we have testified about God that he raised Christ from the dead. But he did not raise him if in fact the dead are not raised. (1 Corinthians chapter 15, verses 14-15)

Some will suggest that it doesn't really matter if Jesus was physically raised to life. They'll say all that matters is that we keep the 'idea of Christ' alive. But this is not the thinking of the earliest witnesses. They weren't interested in simply keeping his memory alive. They wanted to give people the evidence for his bodily resurrection. If Jesus wasn't raised from the dead, then the early Christians were liars who perpetuated myths about Jesus and brainwashed people with ridiculous notions. If it didn't happen, then it's futile for me to believe that it did—and I will have wasted much of my life trying to persuade others that Jesus is alive.

It would be crazy for me to base my life on a fantasy story. There's no point in hoping for a fictional heaven. As I lay in hospital, I didn't need a gripping novel—I needed to read over the claims that Jesus had been raised from the dead. If there is no resurrection from the dead, then I should take these words seriously:

> If the dead are not raised, "Let us eat and drink, for tomorrow we die." (1 Corinthians chapter 15, verse 32)

That's right. There's no point wasting my life on God or Jesus, hoping for resurrection and a life beyond the grave, if they don't exist. In that case I may as well simply enjoy what I have now, because that's all there is. And, since I have cancer, it's unlikely to last very long.

There's no place for pretending or fudging the facts when it comes to hope beyond death. This would be worse than buying snake oil to cure cancer, which would only waste money and increase pain. We should only hope in Jesus Christ if the evidence points to his resurrection as being something that really happened. I'm persuaded that the evidence is compelling—so let's look at that evidence now.

Evidence for Jesus' resurrection

Each of the four New Testament gospels—Matthew, Mark, Luke, and John—records Jesus' resurrection. When I first read them I assumed that the authors had collaborated to come up with their stories and that, taken together, the four gospels constituted one piece of evidence. But, in fact, historians acknowledge the independence of these accounts. The basic record of Jesus dying and rising is consistent in each of the four, but each testimony contains slightly different details. And this is exactly what we should expect from eyewitnesses who are reporting a real incident.

Some years back I was subpoenaed to appear as a witness in a court case involving the alleged theft of two motor vehicles. A friend and I had noticed someone driving a car that appeared to be stolen. It had a smashed side window and the driver looked suspicious. We called the police, followed the vehicle, and assisted in the apprehension of the driver. We weren't the only witnesses. Others also testified to what they saw. Each of our testimonies varied slightly because we viewed what happened at different points and from different perspectives—but we agreed on the basics. The man was convicted on the basis of our 'slightly different but essentially the same' testimonies. What we have in the gospels are four reliable witnesses reporting on the same events from slightly different angles.

Two primary pieces of evidence form the basis of my belief in the resurrection of Jesus. Firstly, the tomb in which his crucified body was placed was discovered to be empty, and the body was never produced. Secondly, many people claimed to have seen Jesus alive after the empty tomb was discovered. Here is a summary account of Jesus' resurrection appearances, written by the apostle Paul:

> For what I received I passed on to you as of first importance: that Christ died for our sins according to the Scriptures, that he was buried, that he was raised on the third day according to the Scriptures, and that he appeared to Cephas, and then to the Twelve. After that, he appeared to more than five hundred of the brothers and sisters at the same time, most of whom are still living, though some have fallen asleep. Then he appeared to James, then to all the apostles, and last of all he appeared to me also, as to one abnormally born. (1 Corinthians chapter 15, verses 3-8)

We need to carefully consider this evidence. Paul wrote these words in AD 55, less than a generation after the events described. Witnesses to the events were still alive when Paul wrote this report. If we had read this letter back when it was written, we could have asked some of the witnesses about who and what they saw. We could have questioned or cross-examined them to verify the reliability of the evidence.

These are quality witnesses:

- Cephas (Aramaic for 'Peter') was very close to Jesus and unlikely to be mistaken about what he saw.
- The twelve disciples weren't expecting Jesus to reappear. They were hiding together in a room after Jesus was killed, fearing for their lives. In this state of mind it's highly unlikely they would have concocted an elaborate hoax.
- On one occasion, five hundred people claimed to have seen the resurrected Jesus. They weren't simply 'seeing things'—psychologists agree that mass hallucinations don't happen.
- James, the brother of Jesus, would have been hard to convince. But James was thoroughly convinced that he saw the resurrected Jesus.
- Thomas the 'doubter', who wouldn't believe without physical evidence, was another one we know we can trust.[3]
- Paul was persuaded beyond a doubt that Jesus was alive. Paul had been busy imprisoning and persecuting Christians when he had an encounter with Jesus that led to him joining Christians in prison and enduring persecution because he began testifying that Jesus had been raised from the dead.[4]

Today, the quality of this evidence continues to persuade countless people who are well equipped to assess this evidence—historians, journalists and lawyers among them—to take Christianity seriously.

3 You can read about Thomas' encounter with the resurrected Jesus in the Gospel of John, chapter 20, verses 24-29.
4 The account of Paul's dramatic conversion is the book of Acts, chapter 9.

There were other witnesses, too. Each of the four gospels records that it was a group of women who found the tomb empty and learned of the resurrection of Jesus. This fact doesn't mean much to us today, but in that age and culture the testimony of women was not considered reliable in a court of law. If the writers of the gospels were devising a clever scheme to deceive others, they'd hardly have placed women at the scene first. And so this detail provides further evidence of the authenticity of the gospel records.

There is also circumstantial evidence. What about the missing body? Either the tomb was empty or they went to the wrong tomb. Wouldn't they have kept looking until they found the right one? If the authorities had stolen the body, then all they had to do to put an end to claims of resurrection was produce the body. Could the disciples have stolen the body and pulled off a conspiracy? It's highly unlikely that a cowardly bunch of eleven followers (hiding in a room, remember?) could have overthrown imperial guards. And these same cowardly fellows are the ones who, after they saw the resurrected Jesus, went on to be imprisoned or killed (or both) for their beliefs. Would they have suffered in this way to perpetuate something they knew was a lie? I expect that at least one would have cracked if it could have saved his life.

Some might argue that perhaps Jesus didn't really die—that he just came close to death, or that someone else took his place. But it's important to remember how competent the Romans were at killing people. They didn't make mistakes when it came to execution. And the records show that a soldier pierced Jesus' side with a sword, confirming that he was in fact dead.

As I examined the gospel accounts and considered possible explanations for them, I was persuaded that there are very good reasons to take Jesus seriously. And I came to realize that alternative explanations were more difficult to believe than the record that the four gospels provide.

Jesus has something real to offer someone like me who has a terminal illness: he has been raised from the dead. It's not possible, of course, to prove that Jesus was raised from the dead. History doesn't work that way— it's not about providing scientific proof. History depends on the testimony of witnesses to past events. Respected historians—Christian and otherwise—accept that Jesus lived and died, and they confirm that people claimed to have seen him alive again after he was confirmed to be dead. The writers of the New Testament were convinced that Jesus had been raised to life. The resurrection of Jesus gave them hope that they would also be raised, and it was this hope that strengthened many of them to bravely accept imprisonment, torture and death. They could endure these things because they had the certain hope of eternity.

Something must have happened to convince Jesus' followers that he had been resurrected. The question is what we make of this evidence. Some dismiss the Bible's explanation—not on historical grounds, but based on the premise that dead people simply don't come back to life. But what if one person did? What if Jesus did? Doesn't that change everything? Creation gives us a glimpse of the colossal power of God. If God did raise Jesus from the dead, and if he promises to do the same for all who trust him, wouldn't we want to be a part of that? We're all facing death. Some of us don't have much hope left for this life, and sooner or later this will be true for every one of us. Does this mean it's time to give up hope? No! Now is the time to put hope in the God who raises the dead.

What does this hope look like?

As I struggled to come to grips with having cancer, I also struggled to take hold of this hope. The idea of life after death seems so intangible. I know what life is like now, but I don't know much about the life to come. My life has been pretty good. I love my wife, my children, and my friends, and the thought of leaving them behind is distressing. I'm sure that heaven will be far better than cancer and chemotherapy, but what about beach holidays, watching rugby, good coffee, tropical sunsets, great jazz, bushwalking, playing with grandchildren and going out for dinner? Can heaven be any better than those things? Is it really worth putting my hope in things I cannot see?

The early Christians looked forward in confident hope to eternal life, and this hope was their message to others. These famous words from the Gospel of John make it clear:

> For God so loved the world that he gave his one and only Son, that whoever believes in him shall not perish but have eternal life. (John chapter 3, verse 16)

Here it is in black and white. If you believe in Jesus you won't die—you will live forever. If that's true, it's an excellent reason for hope. However, it was probably as difficult for some to believe back then as it is for us now.

It seems to be making a promise that's blatantly ridiculous. Very soon after Jesus' death, his followers were suffering and dying too. What about the promise "shall not perish"?

What about our hope of eternal life?

The key to all of this, as we've seen, is Jesus' resurrection. Death was not the end for Jesus. The Christian hope is not that people will somehow avoid dying. The hope is, rather, that if we trust in Jesus then God will raise us, beyond death, to a new life.

The apostle Paul was confident in this hope. In Titus chapter 1, he wrote about his "hope of eternal life, which God, who does not lie, promised before the beginning of time, and which now at his appointed season he has brought to light through the preaching entrusted to me" (Titus chapter 1, verses 2-3). God's plan has always been to overcome death and raise people to life to share eternity with him. And God made this possible through Jesus' death and resurrection. This is the great news—that there is hope beyond death, for all eternity, because of the resurrection of Jesus.

Groaning

I long for suffering to come to an end. Cancer is harsh, and the treatment often seems worse. I'm not alone—we all face various trials and difficulties. The earliest followers of Jesus were no strangers to suffering. They were persecuted and suffered discrimination and injustice. Every one of us has witnessed how random and cruel suffering can seem. Life is tough, and death is certain, and yet Jesus' followers held out hope for better things. They longed for the life to come.

We know instinctively that this world needs to be fixed. Our failing bodies need repair. Those of us with terminal illnesses might not hold out much hope for that repair in this life, but those who hope in Jesus can look forward to better things in the next. To understand this hope more fully we turn again to the apostle Paul's letter to the Christians in Rome. In chapter 8, he describes this hope:

> We know that the whole creation has been groaning as in the pains of childbirth right up to the present time. Not only so, but we ourselves, who have the firstfruits of the Spirit, groan inwardly as we wait eagerly for our adoption to sonship, the redemption of our bodies. For in this hope we were saved. But hope that is seen is no hope at all. Who hopes for what they already have? But if we hope for what we do not yet have, we wait for it patiently. (Romans chapter 8, verses 22-25)

"Groaning as in the pains of childbirth" is a graphic image of the intense pain, agony, longing and waiting that comes with anticipating the arrival of a new life. (I'm grateful I never had to experience that pain myself!) The expectant mother endures the suffering because she is looking forward to the new life to come. These verses describe the whole creation groaning and longing for everything to be put right.

In the same way, Christians also groan as they long for new life. Christians eagerly waiting "for our adoption to sonship" are looking forward to receiving their share of the inheritance that God has promised. It's a picture of heaven, of eternal life. God has guaranteed it, but for now we must wait. And because waiting isn't easy, we groan inwardly as we look forward to seeing all that we can't yet see.

Women who have been through childbirth and people with cancer or other serious illnesses may be able to relate to the picture of groaning more than most. I don't think

I've ever done so much groaning as I have since being diagnosed, and I've often wondered about the purpose of my groaning. Does it make me feel better or does it just make others feel worse? I suppose it depends on who you ask. I groan when the chemo leaves me aching and fatigued. I groan when the pains shoot throughout my body. I groan as I grieve, and when I feel depressed and lonely. I groan outwardly, desperately wanting the pain to go away. God's word reminds me that I also groan *inwardly* as I wait for heaven and long for everything to be put right.

Heading home

When I was in hospital recovering from surgery in December 2011, I couldn't wait to get home. I felt sad for those who had to remain in hospital over Christmas—it wasn't their home and it wasn't where they belonged.

I have friends who describe camping as God's gift to the hotel industry. For some reason they don't enjoy leaky tents, getting eaten alive by mosquitoes, sleeping on the ground, using pit toilets and going for days without a shower. When they go camping, they spend their time longing for home.

The Bible describes this life as being a bit like camping. It's tough and it's temporary—and it's not ultimately where we belong. This world is not our home. We're only here for a short time. Those of us who trust in Jesus can look forward to heaven as our true home. Heaven is where we belong. The pain and difficulties of this life will not last. One day our groaning will cease and we will enjoy life in all its fullness, as God intended. This is how the apostle Paul describes his outlook on this life:

For we know that if the earthly tent we live in is destroyed, we have a building from God, an eternal house in heaven, not built by human hands. Meanwhile we groan, longing to be clothed instead with our heavenly dwelling, because when we are clothed, we will not be found naked. For while we are in this tent, we groan and are burdened, because we do not wish to be unclothed but to be clothed instead with our heavenly dwelling, so that what is mortal may be swallowed up by life. Now the one who has fashioned us for this very purpose is God, who has given us the Spirit as a deposit, guaranteeing what is to come. (2 Corinthians chapter 5, verses 1-5)

Each of us will experience a day when all earthly hope disappears. Any number of things could trigger this loss of hope—it could be the physical breakdown of our bodies, the loss of loved ones, the struggle to find meaning and purpose, or the inevitable advance of age. But the loss of earthly hope should never bring us to give up hope altogether. Rather, it's the time to refocus, to understand where we belong, to return to God, to put our hope in God's promises, to trust in the death of Jesus, and to eagerly await our resurrection to eternal life. This is our real hope.

Longing for a change

When I was younger I remember seeing picture books describing what heaven was like. These books pictured God sitting on a cloud, Saint Peter ticking off names at the gate, and people wearing white dresses and playing harps. These scenes looked pretty wimpy and incredibly boring.

They didn't excite me at all. The good news is that none of these ideas come from the Bible.

The Bible doesn't give us a clear picture of exactly what life after death looks like. But one thing, the most important thing, is clear: it will be worth waiting for. God promises us new bodies that will be suitable for eternity. This is excellent news—there's no way I want to be stuck forever with the body I have now. When I was eighteen I might have been able to cope with the idea of being forever young, fit and slim, with a full head of hair. But now the weight gain, the wrinkles and the hair loss, not to mention the damage done by the cancer and the chemo, make this a very unpleasant prospect. I'm delighted by the promise of a new body.

In 1 Corinthians chapter 15, we read the Bible's most detailed description of what things will be like following the resurrection from the dead. These verses don't give specific details, but they tell us what we need to know:

> But someone will ask, "How are the dead raised? With what kind of body will they come?" How foolish! What you sow does not come to life unless it dies. When you sow, you do not plant the body that will be, but just a seed, perhaps of wheat or of something else. But God gives it a body as he has determined, and to each kind of seed he gives its own body...
>
> So will it be with the resurrection of the dead. The body that is sown is perishable, it is raised imperishable; it is sown in dishonour, it is raised in glory; it is sown in weakness, it is raised in power; it is sown a natural body, it is raised a spiritual body. If there is a natural body, there is also a spiritual body.
> (1 Corinthians chapter 15, verses 35-38 and 42-44)

Just as a seed 'dies' when it's planted in the ground and takes a new, more beautiful form when it grows, so too will God completely transform our bodies through death and resurrection. He will replace our ageing, breaking, diseased, disfigured, mortal bodies with imperishable, glorious, spiritual, immortal bodies. Death will have no power over us in the life to come. God will ensure that we are completely equipped to live forever with him.

Not only will we enjoy fully restored bodies, but God will also renew the whole creation. The apostle Peter rejoices with these words:

> Praise be to the God and Father of our Lord Jesus Christ! In his great mercy he has given us new birth into a living hope through the resurrection of Jesus Christ from the dead, and into an inheritance that can never perish, spoil or fade. (1 Peter chapter 1, verses 3-4)

This is a wonderful picture of completeness. No longer will things (or people) grow old, break down or fade away. No longer will we struggle with disease, death and decay. All that's wrong with our world will be taken away.

Revelation, the final book of the Bible, gives us a glimpse of this world to come. It's an unusual book, with many strange images drawn mainly from other parts of the Bible. The central message of Revelation is clear: God is in control of all things. Revelation reveals the outcome of God's plans to correct everything that's wrong with our world. Interestingly, the word 'hope' does not appear in the book of Revelation. This is because Revelation makes clear (or reveals) the picture of what was previously only hoped for. The curtain is drawn back so we can see the object of our hope being experienced and enjoyed. Here God shows us what he promised from the very beginning. This revelation of things to come has brought great hope and comfort to many who are suffering, and chapter 21 explains this vision simply and powerfully:

> "They will be his people, and God himself will be with them and be their God. 'He will wipe every tear from their eyes. There will be no more death' or mourning or crying or pain, for the old order of things has passed away." (Revelation chapter 21, verses 3-4)

These beautiful words are often read at Christian funerals when family and friends gather in tears, for their loss is heavy and their hearts are sad. But there are no tears in heaven. This wonderful new order, in which there will be no more pain, suffering, cancer or sickness of any kind, will replace the old. There will be no more heartbreak, death or grief. God's people will be complete, and will enjoy the wholeness of new life in the presence of God.

Taking hold of hope

We can hope in the things of this life, and to some extent we should. We need hope to continue from day to day. Just as there are many things that threaten to destroy hope, so there are many things that can strengthen and renew hope. Those of us with cancer or other serious illness will find some measure of hope in medicine, in understanding, in lifestyle and in relationships. There will be other sources of hope, and they will all help—up to a point.

We can even hope for a cure, and that's a good thing.

How wonderful is the news that the cancer is gone, that a person has been made well! This is a reason for celebration and rejoicing.

But where will we set our hope when the inevitable day arrives and death knocks on the door? God calls us to set our hope on the things to come; he calls us to hope beyond a cure, to hope beyond death. He urges us to take hold of eternal hope by putting our trust in Jesus Christ.

It's easy to become consumed with the temporary things of this life. They surround us and call out for our attention every day. If we stay fixed on the world around us, on the circumstances that face us, the worries of this world will eventually lead us to despair. We can find hope in this world but it has its limits, and sooner or later we will reach those limits. And so God calls us to lift our eyes beyond this world and focus, with his perspective, on eternal things. The apostle Paul had grasped this call when he wrote his second letter to the Corinthians:

> Therefore we do not lose heart. Though outwardly we are wasting away, yet inwardly we are being renewed day by day. For our light and momentary troubles are achieving for us an eternal glory that far outweighs them all. So we fix our eyes not on what is seen, but on what is unseen, since what is seen is temporary, but what is unseen is eternal.
> (2 Corinthians chapter 4, verses 16-18)

Every day when I look in the mirror I'm disappointed. I'm not the man I once was. But I'm never going to find hope in the mirror. Even if I could turn back time and see myself as I'd like to pretend I once was, it wouldn't help. It's not the outward that matters. Visibly, we're all wasting away.

But if we hope in Jesus Christ then we can look forward to an unseen inner reality. God is bringing about an eternal transformation.

We will experience some measure of suffering in this life but, in the light of what God is doing for eternity, it is minor and momentary. There is a glory to come that will make our current pain seem insignificant. God tells us to fix our eyes on what we cannot see. In other words, it's not about what we see around us or in the mirror; it's about the hope of eternity that God has promised.

This hope of eternity is not wishful thinking for pie in the sky when we die. It's real and anchored in history. It comes from Jesus Christ and his victory over death. Let's put our hope in Jesus Christ. Let's turn to him, depend on him, and take hold of everything he offers. We don't have to live without hope. There's a real hope, an eternal hope, and it can be ours. God wants us to know this hope, to take hold of it for ourselves.

It's a big step to take, and such a seismic shift in perspective doesn't come easily. It's much easier to stay focused on what we can see, hear, touch, taste and smell. We know this world—we don't know the next. We feel safest with what we know because this is where we're most comfortable. But we shouldn't be. We've seen how, sooner or later, any hope this world offers will disappear. It's worth investigating the promises of God: if they're true, then we have nothing to lose and absolutely everything to gain.

LOVE

The Bible gives us many good reasons for faith and hope. Both faith and hope are gifts from God to give us our bearings in life. They point us *backwards* to the death and resurrection of Jesus and *forwards* to spending eternity with God. Faith in God guarantees our future hope with God. And, together, faith and hope have a profound impact on life now. Most significantly, faith and hope set us free to love. We no longer need to worry about our own needs because God has them covered. And so faith and hope free us to live—right here and now, even in the midst of pain and suffering—in love.

In the tough times

It's one thing to know this truth in theory, but it's a lot harder to live it out in the midst of crisis. Becoming a Christian is not a free pass to health, wealth and happiness. If Christians are people who follow Jesus, then we need to remember the painful route that Jesus took. Following Jesus doesn't guarantee that we will be comfortable. Jesus wasn't spared suffering. He wasn't promised prosperity and physical pleasures. Jesus was opposed, betrayed, rejected, falsely tried, tortured and executed. I worried about dying before I reached fifty, but Jesus was murdered at thirty-three. And this is God's Son we're talking about.

If there was ever a time when it seemed like God had lost control, it must have been at the death of Jesus—when the innocent Son of God was brutally murdered. Yet Jesus understood that his suffering wasn't random. The gospels describe how Jesus repeatedly warned his followers that things were going to get ugly. He wasn't simply reading the political climate; he understood the purposes of God. In the Gospel of Mark, for example, Jesus talked about what *must* happen:

> He then began to teach them that the Son of Man must suffer many things and be rejected by the elders, the chief priests and the teachers of the law, and that he must be killed and after three days rise again. (Mark chapter 8, verse 31)

God had a plan that required the suffering of Jesus. It wasn't that all hell broke loose and caught God off guard. God was working specifically through Jesus' suffering to bring about his wonderful plans to give hope to people. This was God's purpose all along. God brought extraordinary good out of horrific circumstances. Through Jesus' brutal crucifixion, God offers hope to all who will put their faith in him.

In a similar way, God is able to bring about great good through our pain and suffering. I can be confident that God is doing something worthwhile and valuable through my suffering with cancer. Like Jesus, I have good reason to trust God whether I'm healthy or sick, wealthy or poor, happy or sad. I can even trust God whether I live or die. God isn't simply the God of the nice things that happen to people. He also promises to work through the awful situations we face. The apostle Paul wrote about his comfort and hope in recognizing that God is in control of all things:

> And we know that in all things God works for the good of those who love him, who have been called according to his purpose. (Romans chapter 8, verse 28)

This is not a throwaway cliché. It doesn't belong in the middle of some sentimental get-well card. This isn't a call to always look on the bright side or become a glass-half-full person. It's not a claim to special knowledge that God will change our circumstances and remove our suffering. This is a call to trust God no matter what happens.

If we put this sentence back into the context of the paragraph it comes from in Romans chapter 8, we see that it's a reminder of God's promise in the midst of pain and struggle. This is a 'life sucks, but God has it covered' promise. It's a 'your suffering is not meaningless or random' promise. We may not understand the particulars of our suffering now, or even later, but God has a good and greater purpose at work. He's working to transform us from the inside out, to make us more like the one we follow, Jesus Christ—and this will lead to us loving others as Jesus did.

This was a hard pill for me to swallow when I first discovered I had cancer. It was tempting to think that God had abandoned me, or that he was punishing me, or even that God wasn't able to do anything about cancer. But, as I look back, I can see evidence of the good that God promised. I don't understand everything that has happened, but I do know that he's been changing me, helping me to trust him, and moving me to look outward and love.

Being able to trust God means learning to be content regardless of what my circumstances are. The apostle Paul talks about this in his letter to the Philippians, where he declares, "I have learned to be content whatever the circumstances" (chapter 4, verse 11). Like Paul, I have good reasons to be content because God remains committed to me regardless of the difficulties I might face. The following words from the New Testament warn us against placing our confidence in wealth, but they apply equally to putting all of our hope in good health:

> Be content with what you have, because God has said, "Never will I leave you; never will I forsake you". So we say with confidence, "The Lord is my helper; I will not be afraid. What can mere mortals do to me?" (Hebrews chapter 13, verses 5-6)

I didn't ask for the cancer. I want it to go away and I long to be healthy again. But I can't control these things. If I focus only on my circumstances, then my hopes and fears will rise and fall according to what I'm experiencing. Hope will depend on a good diagnosis, a new treatment, increased wealth, returning to work, a new relationship, or some other improvement in my circumstances. When these things fail, so will my hope. Any hope based on these things will be pathetically weak and unreliable. God reminds me that hope doesn't come from me being in control of my circumstances. Rather, real hope comes through trusting that he is near, that he will not forget me, and that he will work out all things for good.

God offers us hope beyond our circumstances. He offers a hope that is the same yesterday, today and tomorrow, and which will not oscillate with our personal ups and downs. It's a steady hope that does not depend on us or on what's happening to us. This hope rests in the character and promises of God himself. God is there and God can be trusted.

The Bible is full of reassurances about God's faithfulness to us. In Hebrews chapter 13, verse 5, as we saw just above, God promises to never leave or forsake those who trust in him. The Gospel of Matthew records that Jesus told his followers, "surely I am with you always, to the very end of the age" (chapter 28, verse 20). Both the Gospel of John[5] and the letter to the Ephesians[6] tell us about the Holy Spirit, whom Jesus sent to dwell in each person who believes. The Holy Spirit, Jesus explains, is the guarantee of the hope to come.

If we trust in God, he promises to stick by us—these are wonderful promises. As we wait for the diagnosis or the scan results, God is there. Whether they're good or bad, God is there. If we're healed and we recover, God remains with us. If the cancer overcomes us, God will not forsake us. Whatever we face in life, God is present and God cares.

5 "I have much more to say to you, more than you can now bear. But when he, the Spirit of truth, comes, he will guide you into all the truth. He will not speak on his own; he will speak only what he hears, and he will tell you what is yet to come. He will glorify me because it is from me that he will receive what he will make known to you. All that belongs to the Father is mine. That is why I said the Spirit will receive from me what he will make known to you." (John chapter 16, verses 12-15)

6 "In him we were also chosen, having been predestined according to the plan of him who works out everything in conformity with the purpose of his will, in order that we, who were the first to put our hope in Christ, might be for the praise of his glory. And you also were included in Christ when you heard the message of truth, the gospel of your salvation. When you believed, you were marked in him with a seal, the promised Holy Spirit, who is a deposit guaranteeing our inheritance until the redemption of those who are God's possession—to the praise of his glory." (Ephesians chapter 1, verses 11-14)

We don't have to cling to weak or fleeting hopes. Our personal circumstances don't need to change for the better in order for us to find hope. The only thing we need to remember is that God is present with all who trust him. Whatever dark valleys we may travel, whatever threats may oppose us, whatever fears we might feel, God will remain with us. He will not leave us or forsake us. He is our strong hope.

I confess that I don't always remember this. Sometimes my circumstances overwhelm me. I question whether or not I can trust God, whether or not he is able to help me, and whether or not he wants to help me. The book of Psalms in the Old Testament is a helpful place to turn when we experience such times of fear and are in danger of forgetting God's promises to us. These songs express the full range of human emotions, from despair to doubt to fear to joyous praise. I'm thankful for the friend who sent me a message and pointed me to Psalm 62: "Power belongs to you, God, and with you, Lord, is unfailing love" (verses 11-12).

In these verses there are two things in particular about God that have strengthened my hope time and time again. First, God is powerful; second, his love is unfailing. If God were powerful but not loving, I could never approach him. If God were loving but weak, I'd have no guarantee that he could help me. Yet because God is both powerful *and* loving, he offers genuine hope to all who come to him for help. These words have warmed my heart and restored my confidence in God. When my hope falters I know that God isn't the problem—I am. If I feel that God is remote and uninterested, it's only because I have forgotten God. He is calling me to come to him, to find refuge in him, to find rest and hope in him. And God has made this possible through his Son, Jesus Christ.

Better than a bucket list

Having cancer intensifies life's urgency. I can't simply put things off until tomorrow, or next year, or some time in the indefinite future. If something really matters, then I need to do it now. I need to make the important things a priority. How much time gets frittered away doing nothing of lasting value?

It's popular these days to speak of having a 'bucket list', or a list of things you want to accomplish before you die or 'kick the bucket'. Most lists I've seen are filled with adventures that cost huge amounts of money and, to be honest, are pretty self-indulgent. At one point I had my own bucket list. I wanted to ride across Route 66 in the United States on a Harley Davidson. I wanted to catch a barramundi over a metre in length—a great prize for sports fishermen in northern Australia. I wanted to walk the Kokoda Trail in Papua New Guinea. And there were more things on my list.

While I'd still love to do all these things, they're not the matters that matter most. Having a terminal illness increases the urgency, but having a strong hope in God sharpens the focus of life. It's not about packing every possible experience that I can manage into my life. Rather, it's about focusing on how and where I can make a difference that will count for eternity. I long for people to experience the hope that I have. The fact that people are left in despair when there is real hope to be found in Jesus saddens me greatly. Now is the time to make the most of opportunities to share my hope with others.

Cancer is a daily reminder of my own mortality. Because I have cancer I focus on my priorities and decision-making with a new intensity, I seize the opportunities given to me, and I'm driven to use my time wisely. I can no longer live life as casually and I don't take the future for granted. These words from Psalm 90 keep coming back to me:

> Teach us to number our days,
>> that we may gain a heart of wisdom.
>> Relent, LORD! How long will it be?
>> Have compassion on your servants.
> Satisfy us in the morning with your unfailing love,
>> that we may sing for joy and be glad all our days.
> Make us glad for as many days as you have afflicted us,
>> for as many years as we have seen trouble.
>> (Psalm 90, verses 12-15)

I used to think that I had all the time in the world—enough time to get around to anything and everything I wanted to do. But then I grew older and life seemed to speed up. At the age of forty-nine I worried that my life was slipping away. If a mid-life crisis is confronting the reality that you *can't* and *won't* do everything you planned, then terminal illness is this reality plugged into an amplifier. Now I need to be much clearer about my priorities and concentrate on the things that God cares about.

My prayer is that God will teach me to number my days, to make the most of each day he gives me, and that I will thank him for these days—whatever they may hold. It's easy to dwell on the negatives, to be miserable, to be filled with self-pity—but all any of that does is distract me from the one true source of satisfaction and joy. Psalm 90 gives me sound advice. I talk to God, let him know how I'm feeling, and ask him to be compassionate with me. I call on God to satisfy me with his faithful love and to enable me to find real joy, every day, whatever my circumstances. As I learn to do this, I worry less about myself and am better equipped to love and care for others.

Love is

God created us to express love, but in many ways love doesn't come naturally to us. We find it difficult to see beyond ourselves. God can change this by giving us the power to love. He calls us to love because he first loved us. God defines love and has personally shown us what love looks like. John describes this love in his first letter:

> This is how God showed his love among us: He sent his one and only Son into the world that we might live through him. This is love: not that we loved God, but that he loved us and sent his Son as an atoning sacrifice for our sins. (1 John chapter 4, verses 9-10)

Love comes from God, and it cost him deeply. Real love isn't a matter of convenience but of deep compassion. It's easy to love people who are lovable and who treat us well. But God loves the unlovely, the self-obsessed, those who reject and oppose him. This isn't love for personal gain or reward. This love is a generous, undeserved gift, and it's this love that God calls us to offer to others.

The wonderful thing about love is that it liberates us from worrying about our own needs so that we can care for the needs of others. Love is putting others first, as Jesus did—even at great personal cost. Love is not being filled with envy or pride, self-pity or self-congratulation. Love is kind and gentle, not harsh or cruel. Love is generous, not self-seeking. We come back to Paul's first letter to the Corinthians to find an oft-quoted and beautiful description of what love is:

> Love is patient, love is kind. It does not envy, it does not boast, it is not proud. It does not dishonour others, it is not self-seeking, it is not easily angered, it keeps no record of wrongs. Love does not delight in evil but rejoices with the truth. It always protects, always trusts, always hopes, always perseveres.
> (1 Corinthians chapter 13, verses 4-7)

These are inspiring words, but they're also profoundly challenging. When I reflect on my days in hospital, the months of chemo, and the loss of so many hopes and dreams, I can see many times when I have failed to love. I have often become impatient with my weakness and frailty. I've lashed out with unkind words when I've been annoyed or frustrated. I've envied other people's health and opportunities. I've sometimes begun to think 'woe is me' and allowed my own wants and desires to consume me.

Sometimes people talk about 'playing the cancer card' to gain special sympathy and privileges. I confess to having played this card on more than one occasion. There was the time I wanted a parking space close to the field for the rugby final, so I told the parking attendant that someone in our car had cancer and needed to access the VIP car park. Another time I managed to avoid helping friends clean their house by saying that I was too sick. These were just convenient excuses to mask my selfishness. There have been many times when I've been more concerned for myself than for others—to my shame.

Looking to the needs of others

The good news of Christianity is that God has already met my deepest needs. Jesus dealt with my sin through his death, and his resurrection guarantees my hope for a future beyond death. I have no reason to focus on myself, because God has all my needs covered and sets me free to look around and try to meet the needs of others. The apostle Paul showed this attitude in action as he faced his own mortality. He was imprisoned for his beliefs and, not knowing if he would live or die, he wrote these words in his letter to the Christians in Philippi:

> For to me, to live is Christ and to die is gain. If I am to go on living in the body, this will mean fruitful labour for me. Yet what shall I choose? I do not know! I am torn between the two: I desire to depart and be with Christ, which is better by far; but it is more necessary for you that I remain in the body. (Philippians chapter 1, verses 21-24)

Paul was confident of being with Jesus after he died. He was crystal clear that death is not something to fear or avoid at all costs. Death for him meant gain—the hope of new life with Jesus Christ. He knew that being with Christ was better by far. Paul's confident hope in eternity liberated him to make choices for the sake of others. He wanted to continue caring for his fellow Christians.

Many of us facing the prospect of death are more concerned about those we'll leave behind than we are about ourselves. Recently someone asked me why I was persevering for so long with chemo. If I was confident that I was going to heaven, why didn't I simply ignore treatment and embrace my death? I said that I wanted to keep on living for the sake of my family. I could see new opportunities to serve God and care for others. Yes, I enjoy life and I have selfish reasons for wanting to go on living as well. But God has things for me to do, and he is working in me to enable me to love others.

If I didn't have cancer, and if I didn't have hope in God, then I would never have experienced the privilege of showing love and sympathy for people in similar circumstances. I probably wouldn't have shared my hope in God with others in hospital. I wouldn't have been encouraged to remember and care for people facing chronic illnesses. I wouldn't have taken up writing to encourage those who are doing it tough in many ways.

God has helped me to use my experience and abilities in new situations. I've been equipped to give voice to the needs of others facing cancer. I've had opportunities to speak on radio and television about the stigma and other issues facing people with lung cancer. I've had the privilege of sharing my experiences at a 'Shine a light on lung cancer' event on the lawns of our parliament. I've been able to communicate the help and hope I've found in medical advances, in the love and care of others and, most of all, in the resurrection of Jesus. These opportunities to love and serve others have only come as a result of my journey with cancer and God.

As we turn to God in faith and hope, he transforms us into the people he has created us to be—people who, like Jesus, love God and others. This love gives our lives meaning and purpose. Our words and works can make a difference for eternity. God helps us to leave a legacy worth leaving—a legacy of love. I have no idea how many days, months or years I have before me—few of us do. Our times are in God's hands and he alone knows when they will come to an end. But we don't need to fear that day. In the resurrection of Jesus, God has taken away the sting of death. As Paul reminds us:

> When the perishable has been clothed with the imperishable, and the mortal with immortality, then the saying that is written will come true: "Death has been swallowed up in victory."
>
> "Where, O death, is your victory?
> Where, O death, is your sting?"
> (1 Corinthians chapter 15, verses 54-55)

7 NOW

Regardless of the challenges you face, the difficulties of your present circumstances or the pain of your past, God offers you the sure hope of eternal life that is found in Jesus. I want you to know the confidence that comes from the power of God and the comfort that comes from the love of God. Please, take hold of God's promises. Reach out to him and find him.

If you're unsure about these things and need help working out what's true, then I recommend that you talk to God about it. Tell God you're struggling with these ideas and that you'd like to know if they're true. If he's there, he will answer your prayers and you can be assured that he will give you the help you need.

The Bible contains a number of prayers that can help us in our struggles. The apostle Paul prays the following prayer for the early Christians in Ephesus, asking God to help them better grasp the hope of eternity:

> I keep asking that the God of our Lord Jesus Christ, the glorious Father, may give you the Spirit of wisdom and revelation, so that you may know him

better. I pray that the eyes of your heart may be enlightened in order that you may know the hope to which he has called you, the riches of his glorious inheritance in his holy people, and his incomparably great power for us who believe. That power is the same as the mighty strength he exerted when he raised Christ from the dead and seated him at his right hand in the heavenly realms, far above all rule and authority, power and dominion… (Ephesians chapter 1, verses 17-21)

This is my prayer for all who read this book and do not have this hope—that God will help you to see the truth and take hold of his promises. I pray that God will give you the strength and the wisdom to come to him, to seek his forgiveness, and to put your trust in the death and resurrection of Jesus Christ. I pray that your heart will be filled with joy to discover that, though you thought there was no hope, there is hope after all. And I pray that your hope will extend beyond the things of this life and into the life to come. I am asking God to be gracious and merciful and to give you a genuine hope of eternity with him.

Life is a difficult prospect for the most capable and competent among us. We struggle and we fail, we face disappointments and heartaches, we groan and we long for better things. We cannot live without hope. Please don't settle for false hopes or short-term, temporary hopes. Take hold of the lasting hope that is only found in Jesus Christ—a hope beyond cure, for all eternity.

If you know you're ready to put your hope in God, then I urge you to do this now—today. Don't put it off. Now is the time to pray, to seek God's forgiveness, to put your trust in Jesus Christ, and to ask God to guide you and change you. If you're not sure how to go about this, then I recommend you find a quiet place to pray to God. You can use your own words to talk with God, or you could pray something like this:

Dear God,

I know that I've ignored you and pushed you away. Instead of honouring you as my God, I've been living for myself. I've been replacing you in my life with other things. I'm sorry for sinning against you. Please forgive me and give me a fresh start. Please help me to place my trust in the death and resurrection of Jesus Christ. Please fill me with hope in you for eternity. Please help me to love you and others. Please teach me and change me to be more like Jesus.

God will hear your prayer. He promises to forgive all who turn to him, and he welcomes us generously into his care. It's a bit like being born all over again as God gives us a fresh start in life. He forgives us our sin, he removes the fear of death, and he fills us with hope for eternity. This certain hope transforms us.

Having this hope doesn't make all of our problems go away. Circumstances won't necessarily get easier. Life can be tough, and there may be more difficult times ahead— but with God's help and the hope of eternity, we will all persevere.

If you have taken the step to put your hope in God, then please let others know. God doesn't want us to attempt to go it alone. It's helpful to connect with other Christians. If you don't know anyone, then the publishers of this book would love to do all they can to put you in touch with Christians who can support and encourage you. Please make contact with them via the details at the back of this book.

You might be thinking that I'm somehow different from you—that I have faith and you don't. Perhaps you even wish you had my faith. But it's not my faith that matters—it's who and what I've put my faith in. There's nothing remarkable about my faith. Sometimes it's weak and sometimes it wavers. But Jesus is not weak and Jesus never wavers. He can be trusted.

If you're not yet convinced about the hope God offers but you're willing to keep investigating, then I urge you to do this. The best way to begin is to read what the Bible has to say about Jesus. If you don't have a Bible, you can start reading it online right away. All of the Bible quotations in this book are from a translation called the New International Version, which you can read at www.biblica.com/bible/browse-books/. You can also find a modern translation of the Bible in most bookshops, and they're easy to order online.

I recommend you begin by reading one of the four gospel accounts of Jesus Christ's life, death and resurrection. The gospels—Matthew, Mark, Luke, and John—are the four books at the beginning of the New Testament. As you read one of these gospels, ask yourself these three questions:

1. Who is Jesus?

2. What did he say and do?

3. How should I respond to him?

These could be three of the most significant questions you ever ask.

If you'd like to find out why we can know that what we read in the gospel accounts is really what happened, I highly recommend a short booklet by Andrew Errington called *Can We Trust What the Gospels Say about Jesus?* It's only 32 pages long, but it takes a careful and balanced look at some of the big questions and the evidence surrounding the history of Jesus.

For a longer but very readable look at the basic questions about God—like 'Does he exist?' and 'What difference does he make to my life?'—I suggest *Naked God* by Martin Ayers. Martin, a former lawyer, provides a good opportunity for you to ask the awkward questions, sift through the evidence, and find out what it uncovers.

Both of these are readily available from the publishers of this book—again, you can find their details at the back of this book.

Please take this opportunity to find answers. Too many people put off asking the big questions—about life and death, God and Jesus, hope and eternity—until it's too late. Now is the time. Please don't delay and miss out on all that God has promised—even hope beyond cure.

AFTERWORD

It's been a number of months since I finished writing this book, and a lot has happened during that time. Two different scans have shown that my lung tumour has shrunk to the point where it cannot be seen. Doctors now say that my status is NED (no evidence of disease). This doesn't mean I no longer have cancer—it just means they cannot see it with their imaging devices. My oncologist will not say I've been cured and, in fact, he assumes I still have active cancer cells in my body. I continue the three-weekly courses of chemotherapy on the assumption that cancer cells are present. My medical future remains unclear. The chemo continues to take its toll. I may never be able to say for certain that I am cured of cancer. But there is one thing I do know for sure: because of Jesus, I have a hope beyond cure that nothing can take away.

 matthiasmedia

Matthias Media is an independent Christian publishing company based in Sydney, Australia. To browse our online catalogue, access samples and free downloads, and find more information about our resources, visit our website:

www.matthiasmedia.com

How to buy our resources

1. Direct from us over the internet:
   – in the US: www.matthiasmedia.com
   – in Australia and the rest of the world:
     www.matthiasmedia.com.au

2. Direct from us by phone:
   – in the US: 1 866 407 4530
   – in Australia: 1300 051 220
   – international: +61 2 9233 4627

3. Through a range of outlets in various parts of the world. Visit **www.matthiasmedia.com/contact** for details about recommended retailers in your part of the world, including www.thegoodbook.co.uk in the United Kingdom.

4. Trade enquiries can be addressed to:
   – in the US and Canada: sales@matthiasmedia.com
   – in Australia and the rest of the world:
     sales@matthiasmedia.com.au